OFFICIAL

Updated
Second Edition

T0372764

Activity Book 3
with Online Resources
British English

Caroline Nixon & Michael Tomlinson

Cambridge University Press
www.cambridge.org/elt

Cambridge Assessment English
www.cambridgeenglish.org

Information on this title: www.cambridge.org/9781316628768

© Cambridge University Press 2008, 2015, 2017

First published 2008
Second edition 2015
Updated second edition 2017

20 19 18 17

Printed in Dubai by Oriental Press

A catalogue record for this publication is available from the British Library

ISBN 978-1-316-62876-8 Activity Book with Online Resources 3
ISBN 978-1-316-62768-6 Pupil's Book 3
ISBN 978-1-316-62787-7 Teacher's Book 3
ISBN 978-1-316-62898-0 Class Audio CDs 3
ISBN 978-1-316-62945-1 Teacher's Resource Book with Online Audio 3
ISBN 978-1-316-62862-1 Flashcards 3 (pack of 109)
ISBN 978-1-316-62978-9 Interactive DVD with Teacher's Booklet 3 (PAL/NTSC)
ISBN 978-1-316-62854-6 Language Portfolio 3
ISBN 978-1-316-62869-0 Posters 3
ISBN 978-1-316-62801-0 Presentation Plus 3

Additional resources for this publication at www.cambridge.org/kidsbox

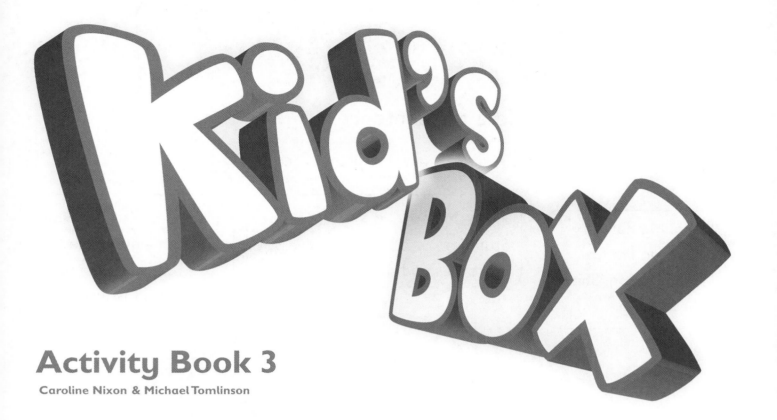

Kid's Box

Activity Book 3

Caroline Nixon & Michael Tomlinson

Hello!

1 Read and complete the sentences.

| reading | ~~name's~~ | I'm | nine | sister | comic |

Hello. My name's Suzy Star. I'm five. I've got a dog. She's called Dotty.

a Hello. My _name's_ Stella Star. I'm _____ . I've got a brother and a _____ .

b Hi. _____ Simon Star. I'm eight. I like _____ comics. This is my favourite _____ .

2 Now draw and write about you.

Hi. My name's _____ .
I'm _____ .
I've got a _____ .
_____ called
_____ .
I like _____ .
This is my favourite
_____ .

3 Look and colour.

twenty – grey   eighteen – red   fifteen – green
ten – brown   nineteen – blue   sixteen – purple
fourteen – white   twelve – black   seventeen – orange
thirteen – yellow   eleven – pink

4 Listen and write.

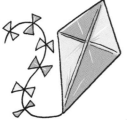  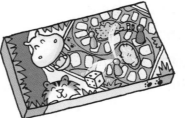 

1 14 kites   5 _____
2 _____   6 _____
3 _____   7 _____
4 _____   8 _____

5 Match and write.

1 ..Simon..

Simon   Stella   Suzy

Meera   Lenny   Alex

2 ----------------

3 ----------------

4 ----------------

5 ----------------

6 ----------------

6 Now answer the questions.

| No, he isn't. | Yes, he is. | ~~Yes, she is.~~ |
| No, she isn't. | Yes, he is. | No, she isn't. |

1 Is Meera riding a bike?   Yes, she is. ----------
2 Is Stella painting?   ----------------------
3 Is Lenny hitting a ball?   ----------------------
4 Is Suzy reading?   ----------------------
5 Is Simon playing a computer game? --------------------
6 Is Alex kicking a ball?   ----------------------

7 Read and match.

1 Is Lily reading?   a No, he's drinking.
2 Where's the kite?   b No, I've got a brother.
3 Have you got a sister?   c She's eating an ice cream.
4 Is Jim eating?   d It's under the bed.
5 What's Daisy eating?   e Yes. She loves books.

8 Read, write and colour.

Jane, Fred, Vicky, Paul, Sally, Mary and Jim are in the park now. Sally's riding a black bike. Fred's flying a big orange kite. Mary's playing football with a small brown dog. The dog's getting the purple ball. Jim's sitting with a fat grey dog. Vicky likes dogs. She's taking photographs with a green camera. Paul's playing hockey with his cousin, Jane. She's wearing a new yellow T-shirt and old blue jeans.

Sally

9 Look at the picture. Correct the sentences.

1 Paul's flying a kite.
No. Fred's flying a kite.

2 Mary's got a camera.
----

3 Jim's playing hockey.
----

4 Vicky's got a bike.
----

5 Fred and Sally have got dogs.
----

6 Jane's getting the ball.
----

09 Match the rhyming words. Listen, check and say.

CD1

1 red   ___e___
2 sock   _____
3 door   _____
4 pink   _____
5 like   _____
6 blue   _____
7 kite   _____
8 train   _____
9 fly   _____
10 say   _____

a) drink
b) bike
c) white
d) my
e) head
f) grey
g) clock
h) floor
i) you
j) plane

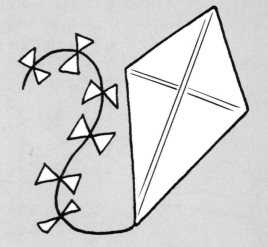

 Read and complete the table.

My friends are called Peter and Daisy. Peter can ride a bike, but he can't swim. He can play the piano and he can play badminton. Daisy can ride a bike, swim and play the piano. She can't play badminton.

Name	_____Peter_____	_____Daisy_____
Ride a bike		✓
Swim	✗	
Play the piano		
Play badminton		

Now write about your friends.

My friends _____

_____

_____

_____

12 🔊 CD1 11 Listen and join.

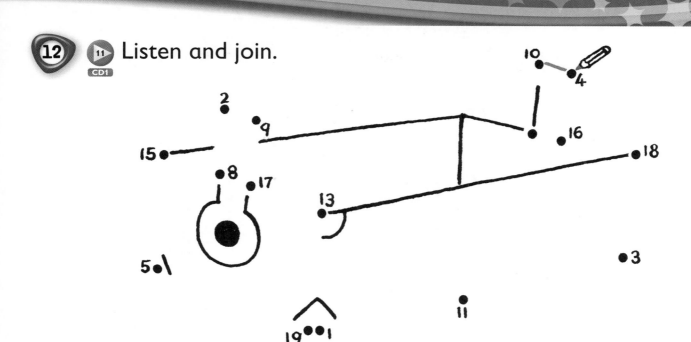

What's this? _____

13 Complete and answer.

1 What's your favourite comic called?
_____

2 What's your favourite toy?
_____

3 What's your favourite sport?
_____

4 What's your favourite colour?
_____

5 What's your favourite animal?
_____

6 What's your favourite _____?
_____

Ha! Ha! Ha!

You've got five apples in one hand and eight apples in the other hand. What have you got?

JOKE BOX

Big hands.

1 Family matters

1 🔊 13 CD1 Listen and match.

a b c d e f

e

2 Now complete the sentences.

son	daughter	parents	granddaughters
aunt	~~grandparents~~	uncle	grandson

1 The people on the bus are Stella's __grandparents__ .
2 Grandma Star's _____ is on the bike.
3 The girls in the boat are Grandpa Star's _____ .
4 The woman in the helicopter is Grandma Star's _____ .
5 The boy on the bike is Mr Star's _____ .
6 Suzy's _____ is in the lorry.
7 The people in the plane are Stella's _____ .
8 Simon's _____ is in the helicopter.

3 Read the sentences. Who is speaking?

1 Uncle Fred is our uncle.

2 Simon is our grandson.

3 Grandma and Grandpa Star are our grandparents.

4 Suzy and Stella are our granddaughters.

5 Aunt May is our aunt.

6 Grandma and Grandpa Star are our parents.

4 Read and complete the sentences.

The Star family are doing different things. Suzy's in the living room. She's drawing a picture of her uncle Fred. He's sleeping on the sofa. Simon's in the garden. He's playing tennis with his aunt May. She loves playing tennis with him because he's very good at sport. Stella's got a new camera and she's taking a photo of her grandparents in the dining room. The children's parents are in the kitchen. They're making dinner.

1 The Star *family* _____ are doing different things.
2 Suzy's drawing a picture of her _____ .
3 Uncle Fred's _____ on the sofa.
4 Simon and his _____ are in the garden.
5 Simon's very _____ at sport.
6 Stella's taking a photo of her _____ .
7 Grandma and Grandpa Star are in the _____ .
8 The children's _____ are in the kitchen.

5 Read and circle the best answer.

1 Suzy: Do you enjoy shopping?
   Uncle Fred: a) I've got a new T-shirt.
                b) No, I don't.

2 Suzy: Does Grandma like painting?
   Uncle Fred: a) Yes, I do.
                b) Yes, she loves painting.

3 Suzy: Does Stella want to be a doctor?
   Uncle Fred: a) Yes, she does.
                b) Yes, she can.

4 Suzy: Do you enjoy playing tennis?
   Uncle Fred: a) Yes, he does.
                b) No, Aunt May enjoys playing tenni

5 Suzy: Does Dotty like having a bath?
   Uncle Fred: a) No, she doesn't.
                b) She loves swimming.

6 Suzy: Do you wear a helmet on your bike?
   Uncle Fred: a) Yes, I do.
                b) Simon's riding his bike.

6 Look and match the sentences.

1 Uncle Fred's got a bike.   a   She wants to read it.
2 Grandpa's got a camera.   b   He wants to take a photo.
3 Simon's got a ball.   c   She wants to make a cake.
4 Mr Star's got a guitar.   d   He wants to play it.
5 Stella's got a book.   e   He wants to ride it.
6 Grandma's got some eggs.   f   He wants to play basketball.

7 Find and write the words.

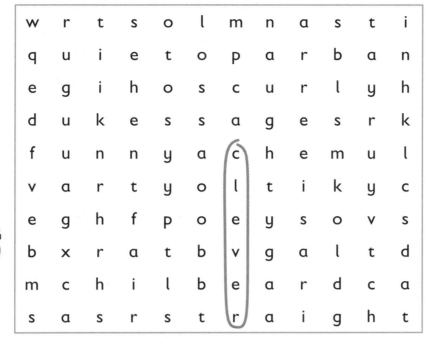

| w r t s o l m n a s t i |
| q u i e t o p a r b a n |
| e g i h o s c u r l y h |
| d u k e s s a g e s r k |
| f u n n y a c h e m u l |
| v a r t y o l t i k y c |
| e g h f p o e y s o v s |
| b x r a t b v g a l t d |
| m c h i l b e a r d c a |
| s a s r s t r a i g h t |

1 elvcre _____clever_____
2 haynugt _____
3 utqei _____
4 rebad _____
5 unyfn _____
6 lucyr _____
7 gittshra _____
8 aifr _____

8 Ask and answer. Complete the table.

Do you enjoy singing?   Yes, I do. ✓   No, I don't. ✗

Do you enjoy ...	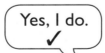 singing?	playing games?	reading?	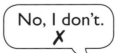 painting?

9 **Listen and say. Circle the odd word out.**

1	day	paint	(park)
2	say	star	name
3	car	train	plane
4	play	farm	grey
5	cake	arm	eight
6	game	make	p<u>a</u>rty
7	May	take	g<u>ar</u>den
8	start	b<u>a</u>by	straight

10 **Listen and colour and write. There is one example.**

results

Ha! Ha! Ha!

What's a quiet animal called?

A shh-eep

JOKE BOX

Do you remember?

 Look and read   Say   Fold the page   Write the words   Correct

  parents ....   parents

 ....   son

 ....   daughters

 ....   aunt

  ....   uncle

 ....   grandparents

 ....   grandson

 ....   granddaughters

 ....   curly

 ....   straight

....   beard

Can do

I can write 'family' words.

I can describe my friends and family.

I can say what I want.

15

1 Read and write the names.

1	
2	
3	Nick
4	
5	
6	

a Daisy is Tom's daughter. She's got straight fair hair.
b Nick's got short black hair. He's Tom's son.
c Aunt Clare's got curly hair.
d Sally is Daisy and Nick's mum. She's got straight fair hair.
e Nick and Daisy's uncle has got short grey hair and a beard.
f The man with curly hair is Daisy's father.
g Daisy's standing next to her uncle Jack.

2 Circle the odd one out.

1
  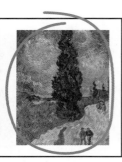

2

3

4

Listen and colour and write. There is one example.

2 Home Sweet home

1 Match. Write the words.

1. fl — _flat_ / _floor_
2. li —
3. ba —
4. do —
5. st —

reet · wnstairs · airs · sement · ve · oor · at · or · ft · lcony

2 Complete the crossword.

Down ↓

1.
2.
3.
6.
7.

Across →

4.
5.
7.
8.
9.

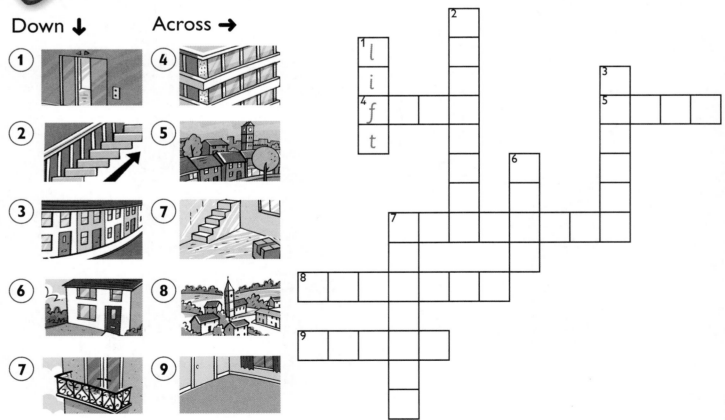

18

3 Read and complete.

> downstairs   ~~village~~   upstairs   floors   balcony   street

Lenny lives in a (1) _village_ , in the country. There are five houses in his

(2) _____ . His house has got three (3) _____ . Lenny walks

(4) _____ to his bedroom because there isn't a lift. The living room

and the kitchen are (5) _____ . His house hasn't got a

(6) _____ , but it's got a beautiful garden.

4 Write about your home. Draw.

I live in a _____

_____

_____

_____

_____

_____

5 Read and circle.

1 Meera's (taking)/climbing a lamp upstairs.
2 The men are carrying/going the sofa upstairs.
3 My mum's carrying/sitting on the sofa.
4 Meera's taking/smiling because she's happy.
5 The boy's climbing/going the tree.
6 The children are smiling/drinking water.
7 Charlie's going/taking up in the lift.
8 The men are having/sitting a break.

6 Read and complete. Match.

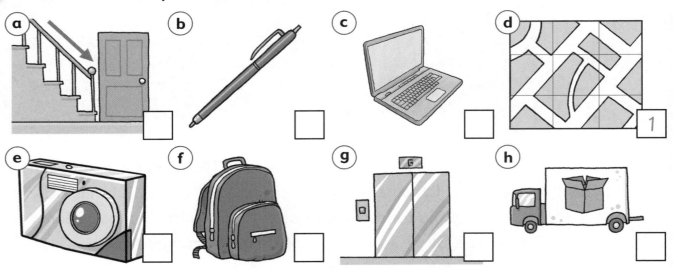

1 We want to find our friend's street. We need a __map__ .
2 He's eighty and can't climb the stairs. He needs to use the _____ .
3 She wants to write her address on the letter. She needs a _____ .
4 You want to carry your books and pencils to school. You need a _____ .
5 I want to take a photo of my bedroom. I need a _____ .
6 They want to move house. They need a _____ to take their beds and cupboards to their new home.
7 He wants to play his new computer game. He needs his _____ .
8 She wants to go to the basement. She needs to walk _____ .

20

7 Match the words and numbers.

1 90
2 18
3 40
4 17
5 50
6 60
7 20
8 13

...twenty... ewttyn
_____ ifytf
_____ etrhinet
_____ txisy
_____ niyten
_____ tihgeeen
_____ ofytr
_____ neevnetes

8 Read and colour.

I live at number 83 and my balcony is grey. The balcony above mine is green. The balcony below mine is blue. The balcony at number 95 is red. The balcony between number 93 and the red one is purple. The balcony next to number 73 is orange. There's a pink balcony above the orange one. The balcony next to the orange one is yellow. The balcony at number 85, above the yellow one, is brown.

9 **Listen and say. Write the words.**

CD1 · 31

yellow	brown	house	window	nose	town
down	throw	out	know	coat	clown

boat
yellow
_____
_____
_____
_____
_____

cloud
brown
_____
_____
_____
_____
_____

10 **Read and complete the table.**

Jack lives in a flat in a city. His flat's got a balcony, but it hasn't got a garden. He can play in the basement below his flat.

Mary lives in a very big house in a village. Her house has got a garden and a basement, but it hasn't got a balcony.

Sally lives in a small flat in a city. Her flat hasn't got a basement or a garden, but it's got a beautiful balcony with lots of flowers.

Paul lives in a city. His house hasn't got a balcony or a basement, but it's got a small garden with an apple tree.

	city	village	flat	house	garden	balcony	basement
Jack							
			✓				
						✗	
		✓					

Ha! Ha! Ha!

Doctor, doctor, there are monsters under my bed. What can I do?

JOKE BOX

Sleep on the sofa.

Do you remember?

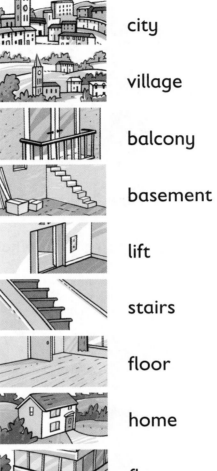
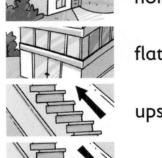

city	city
------	village
------	balcony
------	basement
------	lift
------	stairs
------	floor
------	home
------	flat
------	upstairs
------	downstairs

Can do

I can talk about where people live.

I can describe my house.

I can count to 100.

23

1 Choose and join. Where do they live?

 Sue   Ben   Lucy   Tom   Anna

2 Now ask and join.

Where does Sue live?   She lives in a tree house.

 Sue   Ben   Lucy   Tom   Anna

3 Now complete the sentences.

| castle | house | flat | ~~tree house~~ | houseboat |

1 Sue lives in a _tree house_ .
2 Ben lives in a _____ .
3 Lucy lives in _____ .
4 Tom lives _____ .
5 Anna _____ .

24

Read the text and choose the best answer.

Charlie is talking to his friend Lily.

Example

Charlie:	What are you looking at?
Lily:	(A) I'm looking at a photo.
	B I can't find my book.
	C Yes, I am.

Questions

1 **Charlie:** Is this your house?
   Lily: A   Yes, in a flat.
                B   No, thanks.
                C   No, it's that one.

2 **Charlie:** Do you like living in a village?
   Lily: A   Yes, you do.
                B   Yes, I love it.
                C   No, I like football.

3 **Charlie:** Have you got a garden?
   Lily: A   Yes, we have.
                B   No, we can't.
                C   Yes, we aren't.

4 **Charlie:** Is your aunt wearing a grey jacket?
   Lily: A   No, it's my favourite colour.
                B   Yes, she is.
                C   Yes, it's blue.

5 **Charlie:** Is there a shop next to your house?
   Lily: A   Yes, there's a funfair.
                B   Yes, forty-three.
                C   Yes, there is.

6 **Charlie:** Do you enjoy taking photos of your family?
   Lily: A   Yes, please.
                B   Yes, I like it a lot.
                C   No, a banana.

Review Units  1 and 2

1 🎵34 CD1 Listen and write the numbers.

① ② ③ ④ ⑤ ⑥

68

2 Read and find.

> We're looking for the pet thief's uncle.
> Can you help us?
> He's got short straight hair. He isn't fair.
> He's got a big black beard.
> He's wearing a black shirt.
> He hasn't got a hat.

①  ②  ③  ④

⑤  ⑥  ⑦  ⑧

3 Circle the odd one out.

1 (down)   granddaughter   grandson   parents

2 quiet   clever   balcony   naughty

3 daughter   son   uncle   monster

4 village   basement   town   city

5 fair   curly   straight   forty

6 street   hair   beard   moustache

7 door   climb   window   wall

8 mirror   telephone   lift   lamp

9 house   shop   home   flat

10 above   between   behind   listen

4 Now complete the crossword. Write the message.

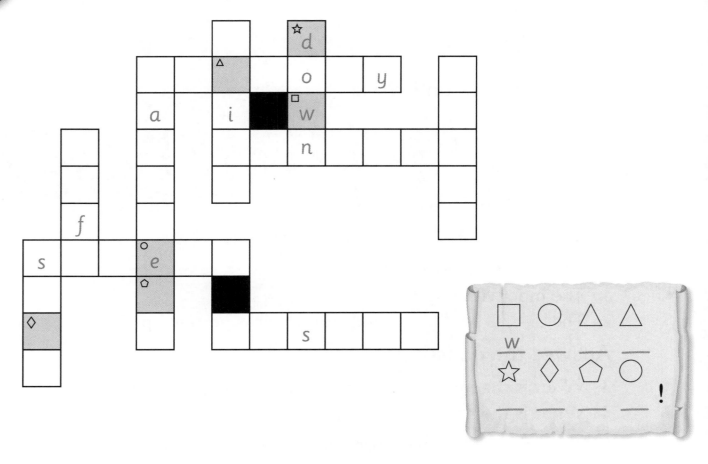

3 A day in the life

1 Tick and order the sentences. What do you do every day?

a	I have a shower.	☐	1 g
b	I get up.	☐	2
c	I get undressed.	☐	3
d	I go to bed.	☐	4
e	I have dinner.	☐	5
f	I have lunch.	☐	6
g	I wake up.	✓	7
h	I have breakfast.	☐	8
i	I go to school.	☐	9
j	I get dressed.	☐	10

2 Look and read and write.

Example   The door in the big room is _open_

Complete the sentences.

1   The man with the beard is _____ .

2   The _____ with curly hair is getting up.

Answer the questions.

3   What is the man with the moustache doing?   _____

4   What is the time on the clock?   _____

Now write two sentences about the picture.

5   _____

6   _____

3 Look and match.

Ten o'clock
Eleven o'clock
Seven o'clock
Six o'clock
Three o'clock
One o'clock

4 Write 'before' or 'after'.

1 I take off my clothes __before__ I have a shower.
2 I wash my hands _____ I have lunch.
3 I take off my shirt _____ I take off my jacket.
4 I put on my socks _____ I put on my shoes.
5 I go to bed _____ I have dinner.
6 I get dressed _____ I go to school.

Now write two more sentences.

7 _____
8 _____

5 Talk to your friend.
Is your routine the same or different?

Do you get dressed after breakfast?

Yes, I do.

Different! I get dressed before breakfast.

Do you have a shower before bedtime?

No, I don't.

Same!

6 Find and write the words.

e	f	n	j	a	m	i	h	f	t
a	m	b	i	s	o	c	p	l	h
s	t	u	t	c	n	k	a	o	u
s	a	t	u	r	d	a	y	u	r
u	a	l	e	b	a	n	k	l	s
n	r	g	s	c	y	l	a	w	d
d	h	d	d	e	i	h	a	k	a
a	y	x	a	f	r	i	d	a	y
y	i	d	y	l	s	w	b	a	m
w	e	d	n	e	s	d	a	y	a

M <u>o n d a y</u>
T _ _ _ _ _ _
W _ _ _ _ _ _ _ _
T _ _ _ _ _ _ _
F _ _ _ _ _
S _ _ _ _ _ _ _
S _ _ _ _ _

7 Look, read and write.

----------------- ----------------- -----------------

----------------- Monday -----------------

1 Peter always plays basketball after school on Mondays.
2 On Tuesdays Jim and Sally play badminton after school.
3 Jack and Mary do their homework after school on Wednesdays.
4 Daisy has a swimming lesson on Thursdays. She never watches TV.
5 Mary and Fred watch TV with their mum on Friday evenings.
6 Paul goes to the shops with his dad on Saturday mornings.
7 Vicky plays football on Sundays. She sometimes scores a goal.

8 Use the words to make three sentences.

Clare Vicky Paul Jack Sally Daisy	sometimes always never	wakes up has dinner watches TV goes to bed has a shower gets dressed	in the kitchen. at seven o'clock. after dinner. in the evening. in the morning. before breakfast.

Now play bingo.

Clare	never	has a shower	in the kitchen.

9 Write sentences about you.

I wake up at _____ o'clock every day. _____

---

10 Write new words. Use the letters in this sentence.

Charlie and Paul never have breakfast at eight o'clock.

1 score _____ 4 _____
2 _____ 5 _____
3 _____ 6 _____

11 **Listen and say. Circle the odd word out.**

1	horse	(book)	st<u>or</u>y
2	box	short	sport
3	door	board	down
4	f<u>or</u>ty	four	old
5	you	floor	more
6	small	house	ball
7	doll	d<u>au</u>ghter	w<u>a</u>ter

12 **Read and complete the story.**

On Mondays Paul wakes up at (1) _____ . He gets up and always has a

(2) _____ . Then he gets dressed and goes to the (3) _____ for breakfast.

After breakfast he puts on his (4) _____ and he goes to the bus stop to catch a

(5) _____ . He never walks to (6) _____ .

At (7) _____ Paul comes home and does his homework before dinner.

After dinner he sometimes plays on his (8) _____ .

He goes to (9) _____ at (10) _____ .

Ha! Ha! Ha!

Why do you go to bed every night?

JOKE BOX

Because the bed can't come to you!

32

Do you remember?

 _wake up_    wake up

 ----------------------  get up

 ----------------------  have a shower

 ----------------------  get dressed

 ---------------------- catch the bus

 ----------------------  do my homework

 ----------------------  wash my hands

 ----------------------  get undressed

 ----------------------  go to bed

Can do

I can talk about my daily routine.

I can say how often I do things.

I can say the days of the week.

Science The heart

1 Write the words.

The heart   blood from the body   oxygen   blood to the lungs   blood to the body

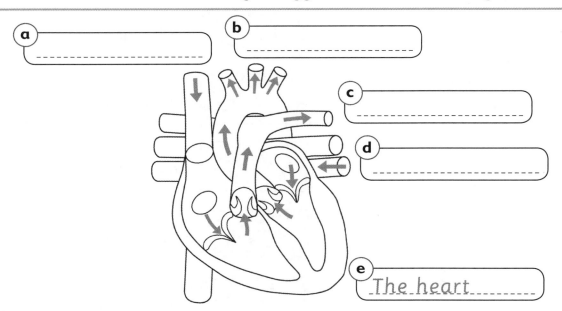

a _____

b _____

c _____

d _____

e _The heart_____

2 Complete the chart. Write sentences.

Activity	Is your pulse quick?
Running	✓
Smiling	✗
Sleeping	
Reading	
Jumping	
Dancing	

1 Your pulse is quick when you run.
2 Your pulse isn't quick when you smile.
3 Your pulse _____
4 Your pulse _____
5 Your _____
6 _____

3 Read. Write 'yes' or 'no'.

1 Your blood is blue.   _no_____
2 Your heart moves blood in your body.   _____
3 Your heartbeat is quick when you do exercise.   _____
4 Your blood sends milk to your heart.   _____
5 Your heartbeat is slow when you jump.   _____
6 When you do sport your body needs more oxygen.   _____

What food does Lily have in these places?

Listen and write a letter in each box. There is one example.

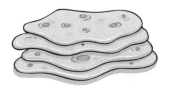 pancakes H   banana

 ice cream    sandwich

 sweets    cake

 A
 B
 C
 D

 E
 F
 G
 H

4 In the city

1 Sort and write the words.

1 rpssot ecnert
2 wtno
3 lhpsotia
4 ukeesrmrpta
5 enicam
6 ubs ttasoni
7 ngubdili
8 aelivlg
9 rac rpka
10 hspo
11 oshclo
12 ylrrbia

2 Look at the code. Write the secret message.

26	25	24	23	22	21	20	19	18	17	16	15	14
a	b	c	d	e	f	g	h	i	j	k	l	m
13	12	11	10	9	8	7	6	5	4	3	2	1
n	o	p	q	r	s	t	u	v	w	x	y	z

T h e r e's / _ / _ _ _ _ _ _ _ _ / _ _ _ _ /
7-19-22-9-22'-8 / 26 / 8-4-18-14-14-18-13-20 / 11-12-12-15 /

_ _ _ _ / _ _ / _ _ _ / _ _ _ _ _ _ _ .
13-22-3-7 / 7-12 / 7-19-22 / 24-18-13-22-14-26

36

3 Look, read and write. Match.

1 You go there to buy food and drink.   supermarket

2 You go there to read books.

3 You go there to play tennis and volleyball.

4 You go there to get money.

5 You go there to see films.

6 You go there to catch a bus.

7 You go there to swim and you wear a swimsuit.

8 You go there to buy good fruit and vegetables.

4 Complete the picture. Answer the questions.

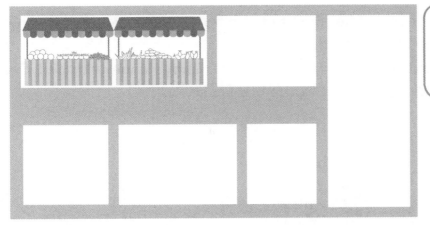

market   bus station
cinema   car park
sports centre   library

1 Where's the market?   The market is next to the _____ .

2 Where's the bus station?

3 Where's the cinema?

4 Where's the car park?

5 Where's the sports centre?

6 Where's the library?

5 Read and circle the best answer.

1 You must be quiet in a
   a) sports centre   b) library   c) park

2 To catch a bus you must go to the
   a) cinema   b) bus station   c) hospital

3 You must clean
   a) the market   b) the bus station   c) your bedroom

4 To fly your kite you must go to
   a) the supermarket   b) the library   c) the park

5 You must sit down in the
   a) market   b) swimming pool   c) cinema

6 To see a doctor you must go to a
   a) hospital   b) car park   c) market

7 You must take money to a
   a) park   b) supermarket   c) library

8 To see a film you must go to the
   a) cinema   b) swimming pool   c) sports centre

6 Read and match.

Suzy must tidy her bedroom. She must put the books in the bookcase. She must put her kite on the cupboard and her T-shirt in the cupboard. She must put her pencils on the desk next to the computer and her shoes under the bed. She must put her toy box between the bed and the bookcase.

7 **Read and tick. Listen and check.**

At school we must:

answer the teacher's questions	✓
listen to the teacher	☐
wear trousers	☐
run in the playground	☐
come to class with a pencil	☐
eat our lunch in the dining room	☐
put our hands up to speak	☐
sit next to our friends in the library	☐
do our homework	☐
drink in the playground	☐
speak English in class	☐

8 **Write. What must you do at home?**

do homework   go to bed   clean bedroom   clean teeth
clean shoes   make bed   put books in bookcase

I must clean my teeth

9 🔊12 CD2 Listen and say. Circle the words with the 's' sound.

1 (city) 2 centre 3 comic

4 catch 5 face 6 computer

7 uncle 8 balcony 9 place

10 clean 11 exciting 12 dance

10 Put the words in groups.

granddaughter   circus   upstairs   wake up   uncle
basement   cinema   daughter   have lunch   parent   shop
floor   get up   hospital   balcony   library   lift   grandson
catch   play   aunt   café   wash   downstairs

Actions	Places	Home	Family

wake up	circus	upstairs	granddaughter

Ha! Ha! Ha!

Doctor, doctor, I think I need glasses.

JOKE BOX

Yes, you do. This is the library!

40

Do you remember?

 Look and read   Say   Fold the page   Write the words   Correct

 circus ....    circus

 ....    bus station

 ....    cinema

 ....    library

 ....    market

 ....    supermarket

 ....    sports centre

 ....   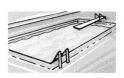 swimming pool

Can do

I can write 'city' words.

I can talk about places in my city.

I can talk about things I must do.

1 Do the maths.

£24   £1   £15   £60   £8   £6

1 Sally wants a ball and a computer game.   £8 + £24 = £32
2 Lily wants a comic and a watch.   £1 + £15 = £_____
3 Jack wants a watch and a kite.   £_____ + £_____ = £21
4 Fred wants a camera and a _____.   £_____ + £1 = £_____
5 Jane wants a _____ and a ball.   £_____ + £_____ = £14
6 I want a _____ and a _____.   £_____ + £_____ = £_____

2 Look at the menu. Read and answer.

1 Four children are in a café. They've got ten pounds. Nick wants a chicken salad. Jill wants some ice cream. Tom wants some chocolate cake and Pat wants some milk.

How much money do they need?
£6.05 _____

What else can they buy?
_____

2 Now you're in the café. You've got six pounds. You'd like an egg salad, some carrot cake and some lemonade.

How much money do you need?
_____

What else can you buy?
_____

❀ Menu ❀

Fish, rice and salad	£3.95
Chicken salad	£2.25
Egg salad	£1.75
Burger	£1.65
Apple cake	£1.30
Carrot cake	£1.45
Chocolate cake	£1.60
Ice cream	£1.25
Milk	95p
Lemonade	£1.15
Pineapple juice	£1.25
Orange juice	£1.10

3 **Read the story. Choose a word from the box. Write the correct word next to numbers 1–5. There is one example.**

My name is Jack. I'm ten years old and I live in a house in a small ___village___ Behind my house there's a big **(1)** _____. I go there with my **(2)** _____ Bonny. Bonny enjoys going there very much. She loves running and catching a ball. I like going there after school. I play with my friends.

My school is in a big city near the village. I must catch a bus to school, but I can **(3)** _____ to the bus stop. It's next to my house!

I enjoy going to the city on Saturdays, too. I always go shopping with my mum. We go to the big **(4)** _____ between the sports centre and the library. We buy our food for the week there.

After shopping I sometimes go to the library to get a good **(5)** _____ to read.

Example

village	walk	dog	ice cream	supermarket

book	park	climb	school

(6) Now choose the best name for the story.
   Tick one box.

   Jack's dog ☐

   Jack's week ☐

   Jack's school ☐

Review Units 3 and 4

1 Read and order the words. Make sentences.

1	play tennis	on	I sometimes	Wednesdays.
2	7 o'clock.	wakes up	Tom never	before
3	at	Mary never	the weekend.	rides her bike
4	before	dinner.	wash our hands	We always
5	do their homework	in	the evening.	Jim and Peter never
6	Sunday mornings.	read	on	They always

1 I sometimes play tennis on Wednesdays.
2
3
4
5
6

2 Find the words.

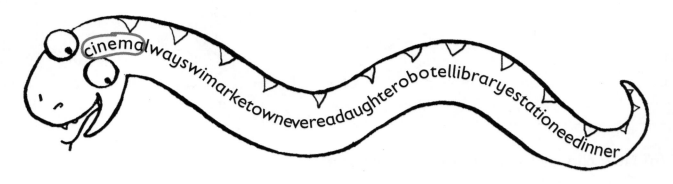

Now answer the questions.

How many town words are there?

What are they?

44

Circle the odd one out.

1	car	lorry	bus	(feet)
2	lunch	shower	breakfast	dinner
3	afternoon	school	teacher	homework
4	Monday	Saturday	bedtime	Friday
5	always	funfair	sometimes	never
6	library	cinema	stairs	market
7	brother	teacher	mother	father
8	children	between	behind	above
9	evening	morning	afternoon	Tuesday
10	never	get up	wash	wake up

4 **Now complete the crossword. Write the message.**

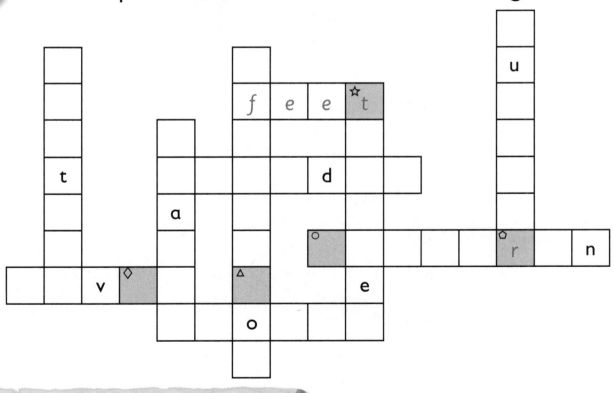

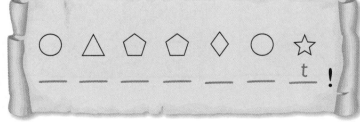

5 Fit and well

1 Write the words.

ear	tooth	back	stomach	~~head~~	foot	hair
eye	mouth	shoulder	nose	hand	leg	arm

1. _head_
2. _____
3. _____
4. _____
5. _____
6. _____
7. _____
8. _____
9. _____
10. _____
11. _____
12. _____
13. _____
14. _____

2 Complete the sentences.

temperature	toothache	stomach-ache	~~cold~~	headache	cough

I've got a _cold_ .

I've got a _____ .

I've got a _____ .

I've got a _____ .

I've got a _____ .

I've got a _____ .

3 Read and circle.

1 My (eye) / leg / ear hurts. I can't read.

2 My toe / back / tooth hurts. I can't eat.

3 My shoulder / foot / finger hurts. I can't kick the ball.

4 My leg / ear / eye hurts. I can't ride my bike.

5 My nose / mouth / arm hurts. I can't play tennis.

6 My foot / hand / knee hurts. I can't catch the ball.

4 Look at Activity 3. Write.

What's the matter?

1 My eye hurts. I can't read.

What's the matter?

2 My .... I can't ....

What's ..... matter?

3 ....

What's the .... ?

4 ....

What's .... ?

5 ....

.... ?

6 ....

5 🔊 **Listen and write the number.**

CD2

a

b

c

d

e

1

f

6 **Write 'must' or 'mustn't'.**

Football practice on Tuesday.

Class rules

1 We _mustn't_ eat in class.
2 We _____ drink in class.
3 We _____ listen to our teacher.
4 We _____ do our homework.
5 We _____ speak English.
6 We _____ write on the table.
7 We _____ help our teacher.
8 We _____ hit our friends.

Play Hockey!

Lunch

Fish and salad.

Catch the school bus at 8 o'clock.

7 Look and match.

1

You mustn't:

play computer games

2

go swimming

3

eat burger and chips

4

listen to music

5

eat cakes, biscuits
or chocolate

6

Aaachoo!

pick up a big bag

8 Now write sentences.

1 When you've got a stomach-ache you mustn't eat burger and chips.

2 _____

3 _____

4 _____

5 _____

6 _____

9 (23) CD2 Match the rhyming words. Listen, check and say.

1 see ___d___   a) door
2 hurt _____ b) cough
3 cake _____ c) fun
4 off _____   d) key
5 one _____   e) shirt
6 four _____ f) ache

7 fly _____   g) do
8 can't _____ h) buy
9 two _____   i) hair
10 time _____ j) aunt
11 late _____ k) climb
12 wear _____ l) straight

10 Read and order the words. Make sentences.

1	go swimming	Fred can't	ill.	because he's
2	sleep	mustn't	in class.	We
3	got a temperature.	stay in bed	Vicky must	because she's
4	Daisy mustn't	got a backache.	because she's	carry big bags
5	must	We	with toothpaste.	clean our teeth
6	with	the matter	What's	Jack?

1 _Fred can't go swimming because he's ill._ _____

2 _____

3 _____

4 _____

5 _____

6 _____

Ha! Ha! Ha!

What kind of dog always has a temperature?

JOKE BOX

ꞏbop ʇoɥ ∀

50

Do you remember?

 Look and read
 Say
 Fold the page
 Write the words
 Correct

 _a cold_ ....  a cold

 ....  a cough

 .... a temperature

 ....  a headache

 .... a stomach-ache

 .... a toothache

 .... an earache

 ....  a backache

Can do

I can write 'parts of the body' words.

I can say what's wrong with me.

I can talk about things I mustn't do.

51

1 Find the 'healthy' words.

h	i	g	s	w	i	m	a
s	l	e	e	p	b	s	t
u	a	r	i	d	e	p	w
j	u	m	k	a	r	l	a
f	e	a	t	n	s	a	l
h	h	o	s	c	r	y	k
j	s	t	l	e	u	a	i
c	l	a	m	b	n	h	i
d	r	i	n	k	r	o	p

2 Tick or cross the boxes. Is it healthy?

Look and read and write.

Examples

There are eight ____chairs____ in the room.

What is the baby doing? ____sleeping____

Questions
Complete the sentences.

1 The boy has got a cold and is wearing a striped _____

2 In the poster, the park is between a library and a _____

Answer the questions.

3 What's the man with the black shoes doing? _____

4 Where are the books? _____

Now write two sentences about the picture.

5 _____

6 _____

6 A day in the country

1 Sort and write the words.

1 virer _river_
2 ldfei _____
3 soreft _____

4 nplta _____
5 keal _____

6 flae _____
7 sgasr _____

2 Read the text. Write 'yes' or 'no'.

The Stars enjoy going to the countryside for picnics. Stella loves looking at plants and their leaves and drawing them in her notebook. Suzy enjoys playing on the grass. Simon loves swimming in the lake and walking in the forest with his map. Grandpa loves fishing in the river and sleeping on a towel or a blanket after lunch.

Dotty loves running in the fields, but she must always stay with the family because sometimes there are other animals.

1 The Stars don't like going to the countryside for picnics.   _no_
2 Stella loves looking at bikes.   _____
3 Stella draws plants and their leaves.   _____
4 Suzy enjoys playing on the blanket.   _____
5 Simon loves swimming in the lake.   _____
6 Grandpa loves swimming in the river.   _____
7 Dotty loves sleeping in the fields.   _____
8 Sometimes there are animals in the fields.   _____

3 Ask your friend. Complete the questionnaire.

Free time questionnaire

1 Do you enjoy going to the countryside?

yes ☐ no ☐

2 How often do you go on picnics?

every weekend ☐ sometimes ☐ never ☐

3 What do you sit on when you're in the countryside?

the grass ☐ a towel ☐ a blanket ☐

4 How often do you go fishing?

every weekend ☐ sometimes ☐ never ☐

5 Do you enjoy walking in the forest?

yes ☐ no ☐

6 Do you like climbing trees?

yes ☐ no ☐

7 How often do you go swimming in rivers or lakes?

every weekend ☐ sometimes ☐ never ☐

8 Do you like looking at plants and flowers?

yes ☐ no ☐

4 Look at Activity 3. Write about your free time.

In my free time I enjoy going

I _____ go on picnics

I like

5 Find the pairs and number the pictures.

1 | cold
2 | loud
3 | strong
4 | hungry
5 | fat

6 | thin
7 | hot
8 | thirsty
9 | quiet
10 | weak

6 Read and write the sentences.

Shall I get a blanket? ☐ 1 Shall I make lunch? ☐ Shall I get a chair? ☐
Shall I get you an ice cream? ☐ Shall I get you a drink? ☐

1 | I'm cold.
Shall I get a blanket?

2 | I'm tired. I need to sit down.
----

3 | I'm hot.
----

4 | I'm hungry.
----

5 | I'm thirsty.
----

7 Put the words in groups.

good   hungry   thin   strong

~~weak~~

bad

Words to describe people	Words to describe people and places
weak	

hot

fat

thirsty   quiet   cold   loud

8 Look and read. Correct the sentences.

1 Jack wants to drink some water. He's hungry.
No. He's thirsty.

2 May's got a headache. The music is quiet.

_____

3 Look at Peter. He's very weak!

_____

4 Fred doesn't like the film. It's very good.

_____

5 Anna needs to eat. She's thirsty.

_____

6 Jim's wearing a jacket and a hat. It's hot today.

_____

9 **35** CD2 Listen and say. Circle the odd word out.

1	green	(red)	eat	please
2	cheese	sea	sleep	head
3	leaf	bread	see	team
4	he<u>a</u>lthy	dream	weak	sheep
5	she	we	help	three
6	r<u>ea</u>dy	need	tree	p<u>eo</u>ple
7	meat	teeth	clean	friend

  10 **36** CD2 Listen, colour and write.

Ha! Ha! Ha!

What can you see in the centre of a field?

JOKE BOX

The letter 'e'!

Do you remember?

 Look and read   Say   Fold the page   Write the words   Correct

 forest.............    forest

 ....   plant

 ....    leaf

 ....    grass

 ....    field

 ....    lake

 ....    hungry

 ....    thirsty

 ....    cold

Can do

I can talk about the countryside.

I can talk about things I like doing.

I can make suggestions.

1 Write the words.

> lettuce   roots   orange tree   carrots   sunflower   ~~leaves~~   fruit   seeds

a
leaves

b _____

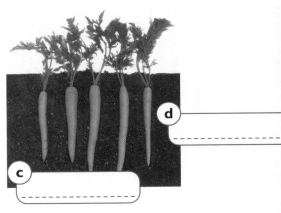

d _____

c _____

e _____

f _____

h _____

g _____

2 Which part do we eat? Complete the table.

> orange   ~~potato~~   carrot   apple   spinach
> pea   lettuce   sunflower   pear   cabbage

Roots	Seeds	Leaves	Fruit
potato			

Look and read. Choose the correct words and write them on the lines. There is one example.

a leaf

a plant

a field

a lake

a tree

a forest

a picnic

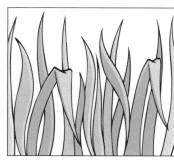

grass

Example

This is usually green. You must water it every day.   _a plant_

Questions

1 This is on the ground. It's green and sheep eat it.   _____

2 We sometimes eat this in the countryside.   _____

3 This is the name for a lot of trees in the countryside.   _____

4 Apples grow on this.   _____

5 You can see horses or cows here in the countryside.   _____

6 This is part of a plant or a tree. It's often small and green.   _____

Review Units 5 and 6

1 Choose your adventure.

Come to | Treetop Mountain / Coolwater Lake | . Here you can go | swimming / climbing | so

remember to bring | strong shoes / a swimsuit | . You can see | beautiful birds / fantastic fish | and

you can walk | in dark forests / on clean beaches | . It's hot and sunny so you must bring

| a hat / water | . You mustn't | catch animals / fish | here.

Remember to bring your | map / bag | and have fun!

2 Look at Activity 1. Write.

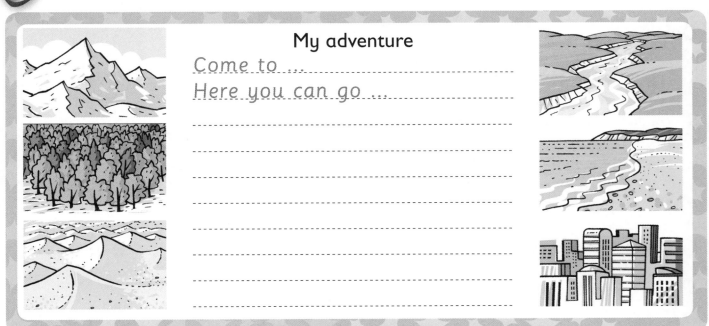

My adventure

Come to ...

Here you can go ...

3 Circle the odd one out.

1	temperature	cough	cold	⟨shoulder⟩
2	hungry	sleep	eat	play
3	eyes	hurts	ears	arms
4	stomach	headache	backache	toothache
5	lake	river	sea	field
6	leaf	loud	good	bad
7	run	swim	climb	fat
8	grass	plant	picnic	flower
9	hungry	grass	thirsty	tired
10	loud	weak	quiet	blanket

4 Now complete the crossword. Write the message.

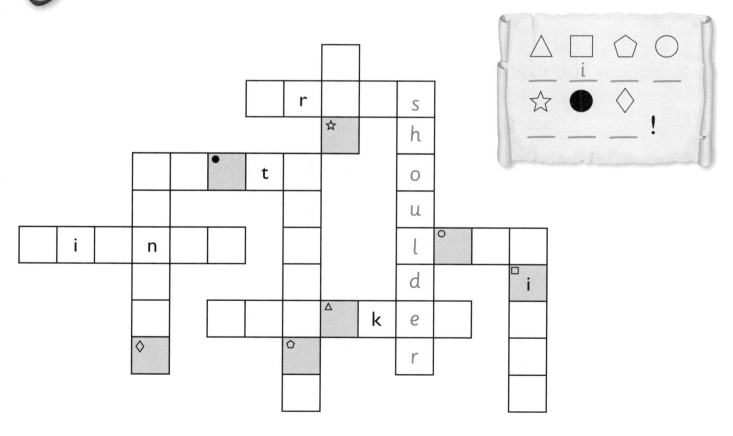

7 World of animals

1 Put these animals in alphabetical order.

1 _bat_____
2 _____
3 _____

4 _____
5 _____
6 _____

7 _____
8 _____
9 _____

2 Follow the animals. Answer.

Start →

bear	panda	kangaroo	lion	library	funny
hospital	clean	strong	whale	hungry	fish
thirsty	dolphin	elephant	giraffe	clever	tiger
long	crocodile	cinema	huge	mouse	bat
naughty	shark	monkey	parrot	hippo	market

Finish

How many animals are there? _____
_____

There are four city words. What are they? _____
_____

There are nine adjectives. What are they? _____
_____

3 Look at the animals. Read and correct.

1 This animal has got two legs and a lot of hair on its feet. It eats chocolate and sleeps a lot. It's a big dog.
This animal has got four legs

2 This big green animal lives in Africa. It's got two short, weak legs and two short, fat arms. It can fly. It carries its picnic in a bag next to its head.

3 This big purple or yellow animal can fly but it isn't a bird. It eats ice cream and small cakes. It dances in the day and wakes up and sings at night.

4 Write about your favourite wild animal.

My favourite wild animal is

5 Read and circle.

1 Kangaroos are smaller / (bigger) than bats.
2 Crocodiles are shorter / longer than lizards.
3 Parrots are quieter / louder than mice.
4 Horses are quicker / slower than cows.
5 Giraffes are shorter / taller than hippos.
6 Bears are stronger / weaker than monkeys.

6 Look at the picture. Read and write 'yes' or 'no'.

1 The bear's cleaner than the monkey.
   _yes_____

2 The bear's sadder than the monkey.
   ----

3 The bear's hungrier than the monkey.
   ----

4 The monkey's hotter than the bear.
   ----

5 The monkey's dirtier than the bear.
   ----

6 The bear's happier than the monkey.
   ----

7 Read and match. Write the words on the chart.

1 strong [j]   a cleaner
2 hungry [ ]   b easier
3 good [ ]   c dirtier
4 dirty [ ]   d weaker
5 clean [ ]   e hungrier
6 bad [ ]   f thinner
7 weak [ ]   g quieter
8 fat [ ]   h worse
9 easy [ ]   i hotter
10 thin [ ]   j stronger
11 quiet [ ]   k better
12 hot [ ]   l fatter

long**er**	big**ger**
stronger	

happ**ier**	different!

8 Colour and write.

1 The grey lion's younger than the white one.
2
3
4
5
6

9 🔊 **08** **CD3** **Listen and say. Complete the words.**

1 a dol_ph_in   2 a ____rog   3 a ____oto   4 a ____armer

5 an ele____ant   6 a ____ield   7 ____ruit   8 a ____one

10 **Sort and write the words.**

1	tberet	b_etter_____
2	geibgr	b_____
3	tedirir	d_____
4	ireeas	e_____
5	rodle	o_____
6	rtqiuee	q_____
7	lsalmre	s_____
8	gonsterr	s_____
9	sower	w_____
10	tefart	f_____

11 **Now find the words.**

r	d	u	j	m	o	l	d	e	r
b	i	g	g	e	r	r	t	g	e
m	r	x	w	p	m	j	i	q	a
s	t	r	o	n	g	e	r	u	s
e	i	e	r	t	q	f	a	i	i
b	e	i	s	p	w	p	v	e	e
x	r	o	e	u	m	i	a	t	r
s	m	a	l	l	e	r	b	e	o
s	j	q	f	a	t	t	e	r	n
b	e	t	t	e	r	a	g	b	s

 Ha! Ha! Ha!

 JOKE BOX

What do lions call smaller animals?

¡ooⅎ

Do you remember?

 Look and read   Say   Fold the page   Write the words   Correct

 *panda* _____   panda

 _____   kangaroo

 _____   dolphin

 _____    whale

 _____   shark

 _____   penguin

 _____   lion

 _____   bear

 _____   parrot

Can do

I can talk about wild animals.

I can talk about where animals live and what they eat.

I can compare things.

1 Sort and write the words.

1
avec

2
legunj

3
flawterla

4
nimotuna

5
korc

6
nisald

1 _cave_ _ _ _ _ _ _ _ _ _ _ _   2 _ _ _ _ _ _ _ _ _ _ _ _   3 _ _ _ _ _ _ _ _ _ _ _ _

4 _ _ _ _ _ _ _ _ _ _ _ _   5 _ _ _ _ _ _ _ _ _ _ _ _   6 _ _ _ _ _ _ _ _ _ _ _ _

2   Listen. Write the words.

~~monkey~~   bear   bat   dolphin   snake   parrot   lizard   shark

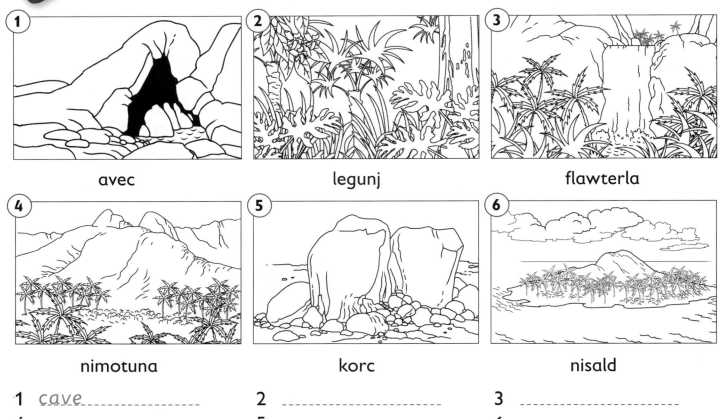

a _monkey_ _ _ _ _

b _ _ _ _ _ _ _ _ _ _ _

c _ _ _ _ _ _ _ _ _ _ _

d _ _ _ _ _ _ _ _ _ _ _

e _ _ _ _ _ _ _ _ _ _ _

f _ _ _ _ _ _ _ _ _ _ _

g _ _ _ _ _ _ _ _ _ _ _

h _ _ _ _ _ _ _ _ _ _ _

3 **Listen and write. There is one example.**
CD3

Charlie's school project

	When?	Wednesday
1	How many animals?	
2	Which kind of animals?	
3	Charlie's favourite animal:	
4	Favourite animal's food:	
5	Name of project:	

8 Weather report

1 Look and read and write.

a cloud

the sun

~~the wind~~

a rainbow

the snow

the rain

1 It's strong.   _the wind_
2 It's hot and yellow.   ----------------
3 It's wet.   ----------------
4 It's cold and white.   ----------------
5 It's beautiful and has got many colours!   ----------------
6 It's white, grey or black.   ----------------

2 Read and circle the correct answer.

1 It's hot and (sunny) / snowing.
2 It's wet and sunny. There's a beautiful windy / (rainbow.)
3 It's very grey and cloudy / sunny today.
4 I can make a snowman. There's a lot of snow / sun.
5 We can't go out to play. It's wet and grey. It's raining / sunny.
6 Let's go to the beach. It's a beautiful sunny / windy day.
7 It's snowing / raining in the jungle.
8 It's a beautiful day. It's dry / wet and sunny. Let's have a picnic.
9 It's wet and cloudy. It's raining / rainbow.
10 It's snowing / rainbow in the mountains.

3 🔊 **15** **Listen and draw the weather.**

a    b 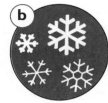   c 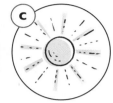   d    e    f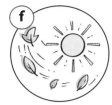

4 **Now complete the sentences.**

1 In the mountains *it's windy.* _____
2 In the city _____
3 In the forest _____
4 At the lake _____
5 In the countryside _____
6 At the beach _____

5 Read and complete the sentences.

| wasn't | ~~was~~ | sweater | were | was | scarf | brilliant |

Last weekend, Meera (1) __was__ in the mountains with her family.
They (2) _____ on holiday. There (3) _____ a lot of snow.
It was (4) _____ ! Meera (5) _____ cold because she was in a
hat and (6) _____ and she had a (7) _____ under her coat.

6 Look at the code. Write the secret message.

26	25	24	23	22	21	20	19	18	17	16	15	14
a	b	c	d	e	f	g	h	i	j	k	l	m
13	12	11	10	9	8	7	6	5	4	3	2	1
n	o	p	q	r	s	t	u	v	w	x	y	z

W e /_ _ _ _ _/ _ _/_ _ _/ _ _ _ _ _ _ _/ _ _ _ _/_ _ _ _ .
4-22 / 4-22-9-22 / 18-13 / 7-19-22 / 17-6-13-20-15-22 / 15-26-8-7 / 4-22-22-16 .

_ _/_ _ _ _ ' _/_ _ _ _/ _ _ _ _/ _ _ _ _ _/ _ _ _ _/
18-7 / 4-26-8-13- ' 7 / 4-22-7 / 26-13-23 / 4-18-13-23-2 / 26-13-23 /

_ _ / _ _ _ _ _ _ ' _/ _ _ _ _ . / _ _/_ _ _ _/ _ _ _ .
4-22 / 4-22-9-22-13- ' 7 / 24-12-15-23 . / 18-7 / 4-26-8 / 21-6-13 .

7 Ask and answer. Choose words from the box.

| at home | at a friend's house | at school | at the cinema | in bed |
| at the library | in the park | at the shops | at the sports centre |

Where were you on Monday afternoon?

I was at the sports centre.

	Me	Friend 1	Friend 2	Friend 3	Friend 4
Monday afternoon					
Tuesday evening					
Wednesday night					
Thursday morning					
Friday evening					

8 Write about your weekend.

On Saturday morning I was

On Sunday morning

9 Listen and say. Complete the sentences.

CD3

| whale | ~~What's~~ | windy | wearing | waterfall |

1 __What's__ the weather like? It's wet and _____ .

2 Why are you _____ a sweater? Because it's cold today.

3 Where were you on Friday? I was at the _____ .

4 What's your favourite wild animal? It's a _____ .

10 Choose the words. Draw the picture.

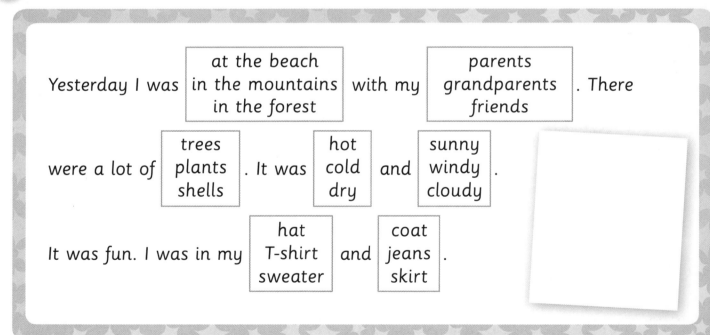

Yesterday I was | at the beach / in the mountains / in the forest | with my | parents / grandparents / friends | . There were a lot of | trees / plants / shells | . It was | hot / cold / dry | and | sunny / windy / cloudy | . It was fun. I was in my | hat / T-shirt / sweater | and | coat / jeans / skirt | .

Ha! Ha! Ha!

Which is quicker, hot or cold?

JOKE BOX

Hot, because you can catch a cold.

Do you remember?

 cloud _____   cloud

    sun

 _____   rain

 _____   wind

 _____   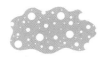 snow

 _____    rainbow

 _____    hot

 _____   wet

Can do

I can talk about the weather.

I can write 'weather' words.

I can talk about where I was yesterday.

1 Join.

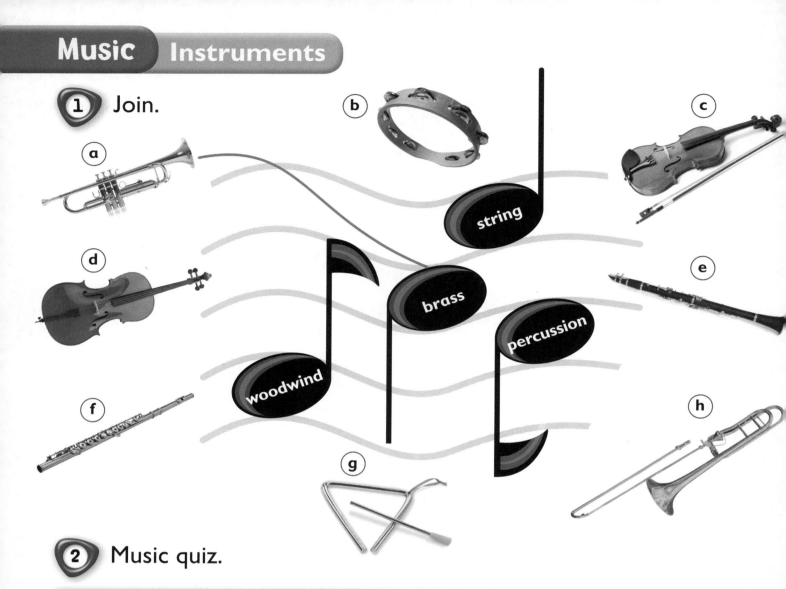

a

b

c

d

string

brass

percussion

e

woodwind

f

g

h

2 Music quiz.

1 An orchestra is
  a) a musical instrument.   b) a big group of musicians.   c) a piece of music.
2 You hit this kind of instrument to make music.
  a) percussion   b) brass   c) woodwind
3 You play woodwind and brass instruments with your
  a) hands and feet.   b) mouth and feet.   c) mouth and hands.
4 How many families of musical instruments has an orchestra got?
  a) 2   b) 3   c) 4
5 A violin is a
  a) woodwind instrument.   b) string instrument.   c) percussion instrument.
6 People who play musical instruments are called
  a) musicians.   b) musicals.   c) families.

3 Read the text. Choose the right words and write them on the lines.

The weather

Example | The weather _changes_ at different times of year. When

1 | there _____ a lot of grey clouds in the sky it often rains.

2 | When it's raining and sunny, we can sometimes see _____

3 | rainbow. Rainbows are very beautiful _____ they have

lots of colours. Sometimes you can see two rainbows in the sky. When it's

4 | hot and sunny _____ people enjoy going to the beach.

They go swimming and have picnics. But in some countries it gets very

5 | very hot and people _____ go outside in the afternoon.

In the mountains it often snows when it's very cold. There is always snow

on the top of some very big mountains.

Example	change	changes	changing
1	are	is	am
2	a	the	an
3	but	or	because
4	both	every	many
5	aren't	don't	haven't

Review Units  7 and 8

1 Read, colour and draw.

Look at the animals. On the island there are two bears. The bear with the fatter stomach is brown and the other bear is grey. Can you see the snakes? The green snake is longer than the yellow one. In the cave there are two bats. The black bat is smaller than the grey bat. There are two birds in the trees. They're parrots. The red parrot is louder than the yellow parrot.

There are two whales in the sea. The blue whale is bigger than the black and white whale.

There's a boat near the island. Draw a man in the boat. He's wearing a coat and a scarf. He's very hot. The man is looking at the fruit in the trees on the island. He's hungry.

2 Circle the odd one out.

1. penguin   shark   (panda)   whale
2. kangaroo   rainbow   shark   lion
3. wind   snow   rain   beach
4. dry   scarf   sweater   coat
5. parrot   bat   bear   bird
6. wet   hat   cold   dry
7. sunny   dirty   windy   cloudy
8. weaker   better   weather   hotter
9. easier   worse   thinner   teacher
10. raining   countryside   mountains   beach

3 Now complete the crossword. Write the message.

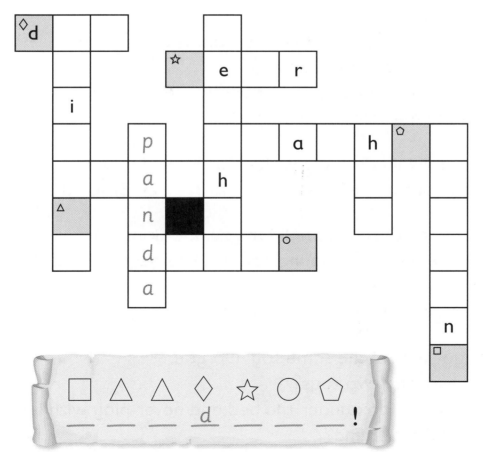

⬜ △ △ ◇ ☆ ○ ⬠

_ _ _ _ _ _ d _ _ _ _ !

81

1   Listen and number.

2 Read and choose.

1 You've got some toys. You don't want them. Do you:
   a) Ask for some more new toys?
   b) Throw them out of the window?
   c) Give them to the hospital?

2 Your friend wants to play with your game. Do you:
   a) Share your game?   b) Say 'no'?   c) Break the game?

3 Your good clothes are small for you. Do you:
   a) Give them to your young cousins, brothers or sisters?
   b) Put them in the bin?
   c) Clean your shoes with them?

4 You've got two of the same toy. Do you:
   a) Play with the two toys?
   b) Put one in a box under the bed and never play with it?
   c) Share with a friend?

Read and choose.

Charlie: Hey! You're helping / breaking that tree, Mary, and I love trees!
Mary: Yes, so do I. Sorry. You're right.
Charlie: Let's play football over there in the library / playground.
Mary: No, we can't. Those toys are for small children / pets.
Charlie: Oh, yes. Do you want to play football / badminton?
Mary: Yes, but we can't play next to the cinema / flowers. Let's go there.
Charlie: Yes, that's a great place to play football / buy food.

  Listen and check.

 Put the words in order.

1 | at school. | It isn't OK | on the desks | to write |

----

2 | On the bus, | the floor. | feet on | put your |

----

3 | flowers in | Don't break the | the park. | trees and |

----

4 | throw your | You mustn't | the ground. | rubbish on |

Values   **Fair play**

1   32 CD3   Listen and number.

2   Complete. Choose the right answer.

> want   win   help   hurts

1   You _____. Well done!
   a)   Yes, I'm a great player.
   b)   Thank you. You're good at tennis too.

2   Ow! My arm _____.
   a)   Do you want to play badminton?
   b)   Can I help you? Shall I get the teacher?

3   I don't _____ to play. I'm not very good at football.
   a)   That's OK John. We can help you.
   b)   OK. Sit down and read a book.

4   Shall I _____ you?
   a)   Yes, please. Thanks very much!
   b)   No, I don't want your help.

1 Read and match.

1 Use public transport.
2 Turn the water off when you wash your hair.
3 Take your bags with you when you go shopping.
4 Walk to school.
5 Turn the television off when you aren't watching it.
6 Don't use a lot of water when you wash your hands.

2 Read and complete.

helping   catch   bags   walks   always   water

Paul and Mary like (1) _helping_ the world. Paul lives near his school
so he (2) _____ there every day. Mary and her mum
always (3) _____ the bus to the shops and they take their
(4) _____ from home. Paul and Mary (5) _____ turn
off the television when they aren't watching it. They don't use a lot of
(6) _____ when they wash their hands and clean their teeth.

Grammar reference

 Match the sentences.

1 What's Stella doing?   a) Yes, he is.
2 What are you doing?   b) He's kicking a ball.
3 What's Simon doing?   c) She's riding her bike.
4 Is Lenny eating?   d) I'm reading a book.

1 Look and circle the best answer.

1 Ben **likes** / **like** reading books.
2 Anna doesn't **enjoy** / **enjoys** having a bath.
3 Grandma **want** / **wants** to ride her bike.
4 Mum doesn't **want** / **want to** wash the dog.

2 Look and complete.   (got   Has   it's got   hasn't)

Tom: (1) _ _ _ _ _ _ _ _ _ _ _ _ _ your new house got a balcony?

Vicky: No, it (2) _ _ _ _ _ _ _ _ _ _ _ _ got a balcony, but it's

       (3) _ _ _ _ _ _ _ _ _ _ _ a basement.

Tom: Has it got a garden?

Vicky: Yes, (4) _ _ _ _ _ _ _ _ _ a big garden for my beautiful plants!

3 Match the sentences.

1 What do you do before dinner?   a) Every day.
2 What time does Peter get dressed?   b) He sometimes plays in the park.
3 How often do you have homework?   c) He gets dressed at 8 o'clock.
4 What does Jim do after school?   d) I always wash my hands.

4 Read and order the words. Make sentences.

1 [buy food?] [do you] [go to] [Where]

2 [you go] [to] [Where do] [fly a kite?]

3 [you go to] [Where] [see a] [doctor?] [do]

1 ---

2 ---

3 ---

5 Look and complete.   [mustn't   Can   must   Must]

1 _____ I clean my shoes, Mum? Yes, you must.

2 You _____ listen to the teacher.

3 _____ I run in the playground? Yes, you can!

4 We _____ play tennis in the library.

6 Match the sentences.

1 I'm cold.   a) Shall I get you a drink?

2 I'm hungry.   b) Shall I get you a blanket?

3 I'm thirsty.   c) Shall I make dinner?

7 Complete the sentences.

1 Horses are _____ than cows. (quick)

2 Sharks are _____ than whales. (small)

3 Bats are _____ than parrots. (dirty)

4 Dolphins are _____ at swimming than whales. (good)

8 Read and complete the sentences.   [wasn't   was   were   weren't]

On Saturday I (1) _____ at the beach with my family.

It (2) _____ hot and sunny, it was cold and windy!

There (3) _____ many children on the beach.

Where (4) _____ you on Saturday?

Thanks and Acknowledgements

Authors' thanks

Many thanks to everyone at Cambridge University Press and in particular to:

Rosemary Bradley, for overseeing the whole Project and successfully pulling it all together with good humour.

Camilla Agnew, for her fine editorial skills and tireless dedication to the project.

Karen Elliott, for her enthusiasm and creative reworking of the Phonics sections.

A special thanks to all our pupils at Star English, El Palmar, Murcia and especially to our colleague, Jim Kelly, for his help, suggestions and support at various stages of the project.

Dedications

This is for Lydia and Silvia, my own 'Star Kids', with all my love. – CN

To Pablo Carlota. This one's for you. Kid's Box's biggest fans. – MT

The authors and publishers would like to thank the following teachers for their help in reviewing the material and for the invaluable feedback they provided:

Claudio Almada, Argentina; Sandra Carvalho Araujo, Brazil; Marcelo D'Elia, Brazil; Gustavo Antonio Castro Arenal, Mexico; Rocio Licea Ayala, Mexico; Gilda Castro, Spain; Ana Beatriz Izquierdo Hurbado, Spain; Ruth Mura, Turkey.

The authors and publishers would like to thank the following consultants for their invaluable feedback:

Pippa Mayfield, Hilary Ratcliff, Amanda Thomas, Melanie Williams.

We would also like to thank all the teachers who allowed us to observe their classes, and who gave up their invaluable time for interviews and focus groups.

The authors and publishers acknowledge the following sources of copyright material and are grateful for the permissions granted. While every effort has been made, it has not always been possible to identify the sources of all the material used, or to trace all copyright holders. If any omissions are brought to our notice, we will be happy to include the appropriate acknowledgements on reprinting.

p.16 (1) L: Self Portrait (mixed media), de Villeneuve, Daisy (Contemporary Artist) / Private Collection / The Bridgeman Art Library; p.16 (1) C: Self portrait, 1889 (oil on canvas), Gogh, Vincent van (1853-90) / Musee d'Orsay, Paris, France / Giraudon / The Bridgeman Art Library; p.16 (1) R: Road with Cypresses, 1890 (oil on canvas), Gogh, Vincent van (1853-90) / Rijksmuseum Kroller-Muller, Otterlo, Netherlands/ The Bridgeman Art Library; p.16 (2) L: Alamy/Akademie; p.16 (2) C: Alamy/ArtPix; p.16 (2) R: The Cornfield, 1826 (oil on canvas), Constable, John (1776-1837) / National Gallery, London, UK / The Bridgeman Art Library; p. 16 (3) L: Self Portrait, 1907 (oil on canvas), Picasso, Pablo (1881-1973) / Narodni Galerie, Prague, Czech Republic / Giraudon / The Bridgeman Art Library; p.16 (3) C: Corbis/Bettmann; p.16 (3) R: Shutterstock/ DeepGreen; p.16 (4) L: The National Gallery of Art, Washington, Andrew W Mellon fund (John Singleton Copley 1738-1815 / Copley Family 1776-1777 / Photo by Richard Carafellil; p.16 (4) C: Self portrait, 1889 (oil on canvas), Gogh, Vincent van (1853-90) / Musee d'Orsay, Paris, France / Giraudon / The Bridgeman Art Library; p.16 (4) R: The National Gallery of Art, Washington, Chester Dale Collection (Pablo Picasso 18881-1973/ Family of Saltimbanques 1905 / photo by Bob Grave. G Succession Picasso/ DACs 2008; p.42 (game): Alamy/David J. Green; p.42 (comic): Alamy/razorpix; p.42 (watch): Shutterstock/Venus Angel; p.42 (camera): Shutterstock/Masalski Maksim; p.42 (football): Shutterstock/irin-k; p.42 (kite): Shutterstock/ILYA AKINSHIN; p.60 TL: Shutterstock/johnfoto18; p.60 TR: Shutterstock/David P.Smith; p.60 BL: Shutterstock/Georgios Alexandris; p.60 BR: Thinkstock/iStockphoto; p.78 (a): Shutterstock/Mike Flippo; p.78 (b): Shutterstock/Heather Lewis; p.78 (c): Shutterstock/ Timmary; p.78 (d): Shutterstock/objectsforall; p.78 (e): Shutterstock/Olga Popova; p.78 (f): Shutterstock/Bombaert Patrick; p.78 (g): Shutterstock/Elena Schweitzer; p.78 (h): Shutterstock/Vereshchagin Dmitry.

Commissioned photography on pages 29, 75 by Trevor Clifford Photography.

The authors and publishers are grateful to the following illustrators:

Adrian Barclay, c/o Beehive; Bryan Beach c/o Advocate Art; Jenny Nightingale c/o Sylvie Poggio; Trevor Metcalfe c/o Art Agency; Julian Mosedale c/o Beehive; Ken Oliver, c/o Art Agency; Andrew Painter; Mark Ruffle, c/o Beehive; Anthony Rule; Lisa Smith; Mark Turner c/o Beehive; FLP; Laszlo Veres c/o Beehive; FLP; James Walmesley c/o Graham Cameron Illustrations; Gwyneth Williamson c/o Beehive

The publishers are grateful to the following contributors:

Louise Edgeworth: picture research and art direction
Wild Apple Design Ltd: page design
Blooberry: additional design
Lon Chan: cover design
Melanie Sharp: cover illustration
John Green and Tim Woolf, TEFL Audio: audio recordings
Songs written and produced by Robert Lee, Dib Dib Dub Studios.
hyphen S.A.: editorial management,